Skating at Rainbow Lake

Story by Annette Smith
Illustrations by Mark Wilson

"These new skates are fantastic," said Mitch, as he tightened the laces on his boots. "You'll have to go fast to race me this year, Ben."

"We'll see about that, little brother," laughed Ben, gliding onto the ice. "Just remember I'm the speed champ in the family."

Mum and Dad watched the boys as they raced around the edge of the frozen lake. The sun glistened on the snow and long icicles hung from the trees.

"It's so beautiful up here at Rainbow Lake," said Mum. "It's a perfect place for ice-skating."

"Did I hear someone say that he was the speed skating champ of the family?" called Dad, as the boys swerved towards him and Mum. "Surely you've all heard about Dare Devil Joe… the Silver Blade Speedster… "

"Oh, Dad, you're not going to tell us that story again!" groaned Ben. "We all know that Mum's the best skater in this family."

"Yeah," said Mitch. "Look at her. She can do all sorts of fancy tricks, and they're harder to do than speed skating."

Mitch, Ben and Dad watched as Mum whirled and twirled effortlessly around the lake.

"I can show you a few fancy tricks, too," said Dad, "but I'll have to get a bit of speed up first."

Dad raced across the frozen lake, bending low as he gathered speed.

All of a sudden, he lost his balance. His legs flew into the air and he landed with a thud on the ice.

"That was a good trick, Dad," laughed Ben, as they all skated over to him.

"I don't know about that," Dad replied, wincing with pain. "I've hurt my ankle. Can you help me over to the edge of the ice, please? This could be the end of my tricks for the day."

Mum helped Dad take off his skates.

"Look at my ankle. It's starting to swell already," said Dad, "but it feels as though it's just a sprain. It's not broken."

"I'll use this towel to pack some snow around it," said Mum. "It should help stop the swelling. But we're going to have to think of some way of getting you back to the truck. It's too far for you to hobble."

"We should make a sled," said Mitch, looking around at the icy snow-covered track. "Then we could push you."

"Hey! I know what we can use," said Ben. "Come on, Mitch. I'll need your help. Put on your tramping boots and come back to the truck with me. We won't be long," he told Dad.

Soon Mitch and Ben returned. They were carrying some nylon ropes and the large plastic lid from the toolbox.

"We're going to make the best sled you've ever seen," said Mitch.

"That's a great idea," said Dad. "A sled is just what I need. This might be more fun than skating!"

The boys set about tying the ropes tightly to the handles. Mum helped Dad get onto the big lid.

"Mitch and I will pull from the front until we get you to the top of this hill," said Ben. "Mum, we're going to need you to push."

"And I'll support my ankle," said Dad. "This is going to be real teamwork."

The boys took hold of the rope.

"Right, everyone, let's go!" called Ben.

Mum and the boys slipped and slid over the icy ground as they hauled Dad up to the top of the hill. At last they could see the truck through the trees. It was parked on the road far below.

“That was hard work,” puffed Mitch. “I hope the next bit is easier.”

“It won’t be,” said Ben. “We have to get Dad down that steep slope without tipping him off the sled.”

“If I move my weight from side to side,” said Dad, “then I can help to steer it.”

"Are you ready, Dare Devil Joe?" laughed Mum. "Hold on tight! This is one race you're definitely going to win, as we'll all be behind you!"

The plastic lid began to move down the slope — slowly at first, but then it gathered speed.

"Slow this thing down," laughed Dad. "Remember I can't steer it properly, and I don't want two sprained ankles."

Mum and Ben and Mitch were laughing so much that they could hardly pull on the ropes at the back.

Dad huddled forward, holding his ankle and steering the lid at the same time. The lid swerved towards a large pine tree, but he managed to steer it into a snowdrift, just in time.

At last they reached the bottom of the slope and helped Dad into the truck.

"The toolbox lid made a great sled," said Mitch. "We'll have to use it again next time we come to Rainbow Lake."

"I've had plenty of practice today," grinned Dad. "I think I could be the bobsled champion of the family!"